SPIRIT OF

THE WELSHPOOL
& LLANFAIR
RAILWAY

MIKE HEATH

First published in Great Britain in 2010

British Library Cataloguing-in-Publication Data
A CIP record for this title is available from the British Library

ISBN 978 1 906887 82 7

PiXZ Books
Halsgrove House, Ryelands Industrial Estate,
Bagley Road, Wellington, Somerset TA21 9PZ
Tel: 01823 653777
Fax: 01823 216796
email: sales@halsgrove.com

An imprint of Halstar Ltd, part of the Halsgrove group of companies
Information on all Halsgrove titles is available at: www.halsgrove.com

Printed and bound in China by Toppan Leefung Printing Ltd

Introduction

Opened in 1903 the introduction of a light narrow gauge railway connecting the town of Llanfair Caereinion with the main Cambrian Railways network at Welshpool brought about a major change for life in the surrounding countryside. Local industry and farming was transformed as a result of this much quicker and more economic method of exporting produce and importing necessary supplies. Passenger traffic was never particularly heavy and that service ceased in 1931. Goods traffic struggled on benefiting from a mini revival during World War 2, surviving until competition from the improving road system brought about cessation of all services in 1956.

That would have been the end of the story but for a band of local people who had fallen in love with the line and were determined to save it. Starting with very limited resources they set about the restoration of the line. The section between Llanfair and Castle Caereinion was reopened in 1963, Sylfaen was reached in 1972 and operations over the full 8 mile line to Welshpool recommenced on 18 July 1981 following completion of the new eastern terminus at Raven Square.

The railway's steam locomotive collection now embraces examples from three continents. Their passenger stock comprises Austrian open balcony saloons dating from the turn of the century, 1950s second class coaches built for the Hungarian State Railway and 1960s-built carriages presented to the Sierra Leone Railway by the UK government of the time. Thus the line has a distinctly foreign atmosphere but with the retention, in working order, of the W & L's two original locomotives and some of the original goods stock together with replicas of two, soon to be all three, of the original passenger vehicles, the traditional Welsh rural railway experience is still maintained.

Left:
No. 822 *'The Earl'* was the first locomotive to arrive on the line in 1902. 102 years later it awaits departure from Welshpool with a September 2004 Gala train. The first carriage is a replica of one of the only three coaches that formed the passenger stock that operated on the line between 1903 and 1931.

Right:
By the time of the 2009 Gala a second replica coach had been added to the fleet. Both were built by the Ffestiniog Railway Company at Boston Lodge. The line's original stock had been built by R.Y. Pickering of Wishaw hence the replicas are colloquially known as the 'Pickering' coaches.

Left:
The railway's most recent locomotive arrival, in 2007, was this Resita-built 0-8-0T No. 19. Its power is clear for all to see during this departure.

Right:
No. 14 is a 2-6-2 tank locomotive that was built by the Hunslet Engine Company, Leeds in 1954, and supplied to the Sierra Leone Railway where it worked until that line's closure in 1975. After repatriation it entered traffic on the W&L in 1978. This photograph dates from 2002 and shows the crimson livery carried until 2003. (Photo Karl Heath)

Left:
For the 2009 Gala No. 14 was turned out in plain black and was photographed at the foot of the stiff climb away from Welshpool. Trains face a gruelling 1 in 35 gradient as they depart Raven Street Station.

Right:
The second of the original railway's two locomotives is No. 823 *'The Countess'*. The names were bestowed in honour of the Earl and Countess of Powis in recognition of their support for the construction of the line.

No.19 'Resita 764-425' crosses over New Drive and heads for the setting sun.

Having passed through the Powis Estate and paused momentarily at Golfa Halt, *'The Earl'* eases its train over the open level crossing at Cwm Lane.

With the 184m (603 feet), summit of the line approaching, the climb continues and passengers are treated to breathtaking views of the woods which extend from Powis Castle over the hillside.
(Photo Karl Heath)

Sylfaen Halt is located alongside the main A458 road. This halt was only intended to serve the few local farms and a short goods siding was all that was required. The preservation era saw a passing loop constructed in 1977 and trains occasionally cross here.

The September Galas have trains running into the night. With the shadows lengthening No.19 glides away from the halt.

The train seen on page 5 leaving Welshpool has been 'chased' (well within the speed limit) and caught pulling away from Sylfaen.

Left:
Early evening arrivals at the halt can benefit from some wonderful light from the descending sun. Here the driver is handing the single line staff to the volunteer signalman.

Right:
The background here is dominated by Y Golfa which at 341m (1118 feet) affords wonderful panoramic views of the surrounding hills and mountains.

17

On leaving Sylfaen the line winds its way through more open countryside…

Left:
…before again sharply climbing to a second summit at 176m (578feet) above sea level. This summit forms the watershed between the Rivers Banwy and Severn.

Right:
This section of line on the approach to Coppice Lane is very popular with photographers…
(Photo Karl Heath)

…with vantage points on both sides of the track. (Photo Karl Heath)

No. 19 lifts its train towards Coppice Lane crossing. (Photo Karl Heath)

A Romanian locomotive hauls three Austrian and one African coach through the Welsh landscape.

Castle Caereinion Station is located a quarter of a mile away from the village located up the hill behind the station. The signal box is a preserved survivor from the Cambrian era. (Photo Karl Heath)

No. 19 bathes in the late evening sun before continuing west.

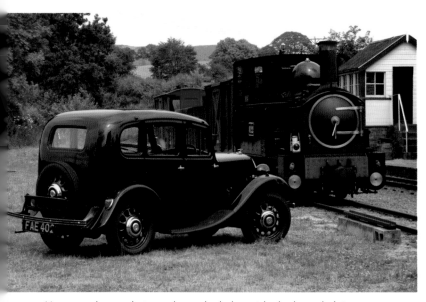

Right:
...after which an
authentic Welshpool
and Llanfair goods
train makes a
spirited departure.

You never know what may be parked alongside the loop, helping to create a timeless scene. *'The Earl'* waits patiently for the service train from Llanfair to pass through...

Left:
On leaving Castle Caereinion the line descends Dolarddyn Bank and heads towards Cyfronydd.
(Photo Karl Heath)

The sheep and cattle pastures of the hills and vales of mid-Wales provide a magnificent backdrop.

'The Countess' arrives at Cyfronydd Station. (Photo Karl Heath)

This particular locomotive, 'Orion', had arrived on the railway in 1983 but required major overhaul and did not enter service until 2000. In 2007 it returned home to the Jokioisten Railway in Finland.

Cyfronydd plays a major role at Christmas as Santa bases himself here and greets excited children that have travelled from Llanfair. He then joins them on their journey to Castle Caereinion dispensing presents on the way.

'*Dougal*' was built in 1946 by Andrew Barclay & Sons Co. Ltd. in Kilmarnock. Much of its working life was spent operating around the Provan Gasworks of Glasgow Corporation. Nowadays it gets to play out on Gala weekends hauling freight shuttles between here and Llanfair.

Having successfully warned oncoming traffic of the train's departure the fireman has rolled up his red flag and returned to his footplate duties. (Photo Karl Heath)

Gala weekends also see a number of steam powered road vehicles visiting the area providing wonderful cameos.

Left:
Just before Heniarth the line crosses the River Banwy by means of a steel girder bridge 114 feet long in three spans. The locomotive trundling across is No. 10 'Sir Drefaldwyn' which at the time of writing is stored out of service awaiting overhaul.
(Photo Karl Heath)

Right:
This scene, on the approach to Heniarth Halt has seen much lineside vegetation growth since my 'Railway Moods – The Welshpool and Llanfair Railway' book was published in 2006.

The combination of the replica coaches and rebuilt original freight stock allows the railway to run authentic vintage trains. The 'Llanfair Train' is seen passing through typical W & L scenery maintaining the rural charm and character of the line. (Photo Karl Heath)

'Dougal' scampers towards Cyfronydd with a Gala day freight.

Heniarth Halt once had a loop line, waiting shelter, and crane for the loading of timber serving the local farming community and nearby water mill. Very little evidence of this former life remains and trains pass through without stopping.

A Santa Special passes the site of the halt on a cold crisp winter's day.

Left:
Beyond Heniarth the route continues along the riverside with the road, from where this photo was taken, higher up.

The signal box at Llanfair was replaced in 2002 and all train operations are controlled from here. (Photo Karl Heath)

Left:
'The Countess'
arrives at the
western terminus.

Right:
A busy scene at
Llanfair as *'The Earl'*
prepares a Vintage
Day freight working.

A vintage wagon adding authenticity to the scene.

'Dougal' busies itself on shunting duties.

Staff and volunteers service and overhaul everything themselves…

...by day and by night!

(Right and overleaf) Examples of steam road vehicles fill the yard as fairground organ music fills the air.

In keeping with the railway's own literature on the Saturday evening of the Gala Llanfair Station is illuminated by electric lanterns for night photography'.

P. & E. JONES
ANDREAS
ISLE OF MAN
P. & E. JONES
Contractors
ISLE of MAN
ANFAIR CAEREINION

No. 14 has advanced along the headshunt to take water.

Whilst most photographers are taking the more orthodox illuminated front portrait, setting up behind the locomotives and keeping the floodlighting out of view allowed this wonderful line-up to be captured in glorious silhouette.

During the 2009 Gala photo night I ventured away from the main floodlighting to photograph 'The Countess' waiting patiently in the sidings.

A pause in shunting operations allowed this portrait of diesel locomotive No. 7
'Chattenden' to be taken.

Left:
The Pickering coaches look resplendent under the platform lighting.

'Top of the bill' at the 2009 Gala was the 'African Train' – No. 14 and the two fully restored Sierra Leone coaches posed alongside the platform.

I do take the traditional photograph as well! This is the 2007 line-up.

A perfectly lit view of No. 14, again taken in 2008, whilst it was carrying a striking blue livery.

In June 2003, as part of the railway's centenary celebrations, an Edwardian Weekend was held and many of the working members turned out in period dress. Here's to many more celebrations for this wonderful great little railway.